Dead Dog Poems

Winner of the New Women's Voices Prize in Poetry

New Women's Voices Series, No. 159

poems by

Lynne Schmidt

Finishing Line Press
Georgetown, Kentucky

Dead Dog Poems

For Baxter, faithfully

Copyright © 2021 by Lynne Schmidt
ISBN 978-1-64662-626-7 First Edition
All rights reserved under International and Pan-American Copyright Conventions. No part of this book may be reproduced in any manner whatsoever without written permission from the publisher, except in the case of brief quotations embodied in critical articles and reviews.

ACKNOWLEDGMENTS

Poets of Maine, 2018 who published The Last Moment
The Poets of New England, 2018 who published How Forever Feels
Sixty Four Best Poets of 2018 who published Aftermath
Royal Rose Literary who published Road Maps
Frost Meadow Review who published Aftermath, and Baxter and also gave Baxter the Editor's Choice award
Empty Mirror who published When My Sister Calls
Crepe and Penn: Volume 6/7 who published Dear Tinder
Monstering who published On How Dogs Choose Their People
Present Moment by All Female Menu who published Kyla
Fahmidan Journal who published Blood Pleas and Library Books
Wine Cellar Press who published Naptime
Southchild Lit who published The Next Appointment
One Art who published The Reoccurring Nightmare Where You Won't Be Able To Save Them

Publisher: Leah Huete de Maines
Editor: Christen Kincaid
Cover Art: Shawn Berman
Author Photo: Meaghan Martin Photography
Cover Design: Elizabeth Maines McCleavy

Order online: www.finishinglinepress.com
also available on amazon.com

Author inquiries and mail orders:
Finishing Line Press
PO Box 1626
Georgetown, Kentucky 40324
USA

Table of Contents

Aftermath 1
Looking for Dead Bodies..2
The New Puppy...3
On How Dogs Choose Their People 4
When He Screams Long Enough A Local Domestic Abuse
    Survivor Gets Text Reading, "Are You Safe 5
Naptime 7
Contradictions 8
Road Map 9
When You Try and Pray This Away 10
The Reoccurring Nightmare Where You Won't Be Able To
    Save Them..11
An Ode to the Cancer that Will Take My Dog.......................................12
Sunday Morning..13
How Forever Feels 14
Blood Pleas and Library Books..15
In The Morning...17
The Last Moment..18
When It's Time..19
Baxter 20
Dear Tinder 23
The Next Appointment 24
Control..25
Enyo..26
The World without Them 27
My Therapist Wants to Hospitalize Me...28
What I Already Knew 29
Fire Hydrants 30
On Being Happy 31
The Last Touch..32
On Why I'm Not Better Yet...33
On Letting Myself Feel..35
When My Sister Calls..36
Kyla...37
Dear Stranger 38
An Ode to the First Dead Pet..39
To You, Before Your Loss...40
With Thanks..41

Aftermath

So then there's this—
>the moment after the storm
>where you uncover your eyes,
>and you survived but
>everything else is rubble.

Your fingertips dig into the dirt
>piled on your skin.
>The puddles around you act
>as a bath.
>And you stand alone
>in all this aftermath.

They'll tell you to rebuild,
>say it's only a setback.
>And when you hammer in your
>first nail
>trying to make a home,
>you'll find it's a casket.

Looking for Dead Bodies

My sister and I spend time
searching for a body
we're not sure exists.

We recount steps,
wander into overgrown weeds
looking for trails of blood
and broken glass
while my dog waits in the car
wagging his tail.

If he is okay,
then I am okay.

The mirror to my car is missing.
The window to my door has shattered into glitter.
And while my sister and I search for a body,
my dog waits for me.

The New Puppy

My mother called to tell me she got a puppy today
called to say what a good boy he is
that he's only had one accident
and seems to be bonding to the pack well enough.
She manages to forget that the adults she has flinch from human contact
that partner based affection
forms a question in our bodies
much like the end of a sentence
you're not quite sure is the end.

My mother calls to tell me she got a puppy today
but the dogs she already has shy away from movement that's too quick.

I'm still young and able bodied enough to remember the dog that wasn't
allowed inside the house
the one that was hit by a car
        blood staining the white snow in the driveway,
the one carelessly given away
        saying, *You can see them any time you want,*
the one sent to the pound,
the one taken on my sixteenth birthday,
        We'll get her back, I promise.

My mother calls to tell me she got a puppy today.
Her voice is animated and excited.
She oozes what some might mistake for love.

I know this, because when I was on the outside, I made the same mistake.

Instead, of a joyous response
I reply with, "This is a terrible idea,"
the thing I wish I'd said in high school
the first time she'd brought a puppy home.

On How Dogs Choose Their People

The day he proclaims,
I want a dog, too,
I shrug and say, *Okay.*

When he brings her to meet me,
I stop mid-step, taken by
the soft chocolate of her fur.
She's beautiful, I whisper,
and she licks me.

In the days that follow,
she finds herself on my bed,
follows my dog and me to the bathroom,
lays outside the door and waits.

He seeths,
She is supposed to be my dog,
and yet, she has picked me,
because trauma recognizes trauma
        and seeks it out.

When he takes my money,
        my prescribed painkillers,
        and his stuff,
I tell him to leave the dog.

When the vet consoles me, saying,
She was sick before she was yours,
All I hear is
        She was yours.

When He Screams Long Enough A Local Domestic Abuse Survivor Gets Text Reading, "Are You Safe?"

The night he wants to talk about our relationship,
I caution maybe in the morning,
maybe not right now.

He pushes, and I relent,
a volcano out of my mouth finally saying,
I've been struggling for weeks
to figure out how to end this.

He looks like I've stabbed him with the dog leash I'm holding,
face color peeling like the drywall in our-
        my apartment
from raining damage.

But he says *I don't want to live without you,*
I shrug, *That's no longer your decision.*

My pitbull senses the lightning in the air,
and moves closer to me.
I take the leash from his hands,
so I can keep both dogs safe.

He advances, finger a familiar arrow
and I see the way my father once shoved this dart
against my sister's chest hard enough to leave a bullseye print.

My pitbull is also a rescue,
she slams her body against me,
asking *Now?*
She, too, has been here before.
I stroke her face in answer, *Not yet, we are okay.*

Still, her body ridges like a mountain of granite,
a linebacker ready to demolish the person in her path,
to bring her football safely home,
and I wonder if only bad people are afraid of her breed
because they've seen her defend her person from them.

I'll kill myself, he threatens between clenched teeth.
And the laugh erupts out of me before I can choke it back.

I have only ever heard this threat as a precipitant to
the violence when a woman stays
in hopes of saving his life.

That'd be your choice, I say.

Because I've made mine.

As we walk home,
he screams behind us,
voice echoing in the otherwise abandoned road
and Kyla wags her tail.

Naptime

I listen to their breath as they sleep
curled against me.
I crack apart my sternum so they
can crawl inside the safety of my chest.

Here, they rest soundly,
bodies limp, trusting
that there is no evil
no harm will come.

I am a statue standing still,
a guard armed with bow and arrow to ensure passage,
and when the time comes,
I, too, fall asleep beside them.

Contradictions

Don't cry over spilled milk,
but if that milk has espresso, sugar, and cost five dollars' worth of bottle
returns on a bad day
and your pit bull jumps because she's happy and the cover falls off when the
plastic cup hits the floor—cry.
Because even if you dig through the apartment
find a few more bottles
look through the couch cushions
you know you can't afford another one.

Obey all the speed limit signs,
unless your dog goes outside,
looks hung over
like a flag at half mast
comes back inside crumbling from an invisible earthquake
and his gums turn pale.

Then turn your car into a rocket ship,
and fly the hour/now half hour/to the emergency vet.

Keep yourself together. Keep yourself together.

Until they say he may not live through the night.

Then shatter like the car accident your best friend died in.

Road Map

There is no road map
that suggests turn left at cancer
and right on chemotherapy street.
It doesn't remind you to wear gloves
or to hold off on that beverage until after
ten o'clock
because that marks the twelve hour interval.
And you can't be too drunk
when handling medication that can absorb through your skin
but is safe enough to give to him.

There is no road map to canceling plans,
forgetting plans,
or coming home early because there was a bad day.

There is no road map to trying to foster new relationships
because those feelings you felt
were just under fingertips
and now they're somewhere under a needle
while you wait
for hope
for treatment.

For anything other than what is happening here.

When You Try and Pray This Away

We pray in the space between breaths,
the space between the snowflakes as they
blanket the ground,
that this thing
this ham-like cancer
will not return.

We offer sacrifices,
broken dates and cancelled plans
three-hour drives after midnight
for money to afford treatment.

We scrape by on handmade foods
because we can't afford luxury anymore.

They caution me
        Hope is beneath the sea
        The iceberg has struck and we're sinking
        We are so far gone—even Pandora's Box has given up,
        This thing will take you from me.

They tell me to be careful with my prayers
because there is no hope here.

And when we get the test results back
they give the cancer a new name,
Terminal.

and they're right—
Like the exhale of a held breath,
All the hope is gone.

The Reoccurring Nightmare Where You Won't Be Able To Save Them

I want to tell you
that when the flood waters
sweep the car away,
my surgically repaired shoulder
will become bionic
smash through the window
and pull her to safety.

I have had the nightmare,
water in my mouth as I scream her name,
and I don't get to her in time.

I have had the nightmare
where I save one
and not the other.

And I have had the nightmare,
the one
I imagine is closer to reality,
where we all submerge.

An Ode to the Cancer That Will Take My Dog

The first time we meet,
you are secured in a specimen jar,
suspended in fluid and my beloved's blood.

We have a staring contest until
the vet tells me, there is still some hope,
that you may not be what I already know you are.

The call comes days later, and
my dog's body is etched with words like
malignant,
       terminal,
              I'm so, so sorry.

I hate you for the first week,
shake my fist at a God I'm not sure I believe in,
find myself praying for a misdiagnosis,
pray that someone else is sick.

But as days pass—it is clear
that you have carved out space in my baby's organs.

I try to keep hating you—
But you start to teach me the value
      in each second of the day
      the meaning in late night cuddles
      the joy of feeding by hand.

You teach me how love can break and rebuild.
You teach me that love can fight
      and fight
      and still lose.

Sunday Morning

the calls come first thing in the morning
while i'm holding a dying dog in my lap.
i silence each call, each text, each attempt to reach out
because though i don't know the exact words,
i still know what they'll say.
it's not a premonition or a psychic when it's happened before
and before that, too.
these things follow a pattern of missed calls
and my phone has become a red alert.
i'm already holding cancer between my hands
as though it were a weed that i could pluck away
and not an invasive species
that took root and flourished,
devouring everything i loved in its path.
the silenced phone calls say
something else i love has been eaten, too
i just don't know who, yet.
so another round comes,
as a body riddled with disease
buries itself into my lap,
into my hands pleading with me to withdraw this burden like money from
   an ATM
like jesus giving sight to the blind
healing sores
making a fucking miracle happen.
but the only miracle i've ever conjured
was getting out of bed in the morning
and as always it's not good enough.
the phone rings again and
i take a breath
press it to my ear
and
hear my sister tell me
she has bad news.

How Forever Feels

I am holding on to a string
that has been stretched so tight
it is only a matter of time before it snaps apart
like a rubber band,
and strikes the hand that is still refusing to let go.
It is too hard to pry apart these fingers
release this grasp
because the last thread that is here
bound me from this place to home,
to my sister's apartment,
to the first place I ever really knew myself and began to sew my insides back together.
I understood how the world worked then,
how gravity kept me safe,
even in those moments where I scraped my knees.
I knew how the stars hung,
why the tides went out and came back
to the beaches even when skin burns in sunlight.
I knew then that happiness tasted like salt stained lips,
and fingertips that interlocked beside fire.
And while I cling to this,
what's right here, right now,
like a child and their safety blanket that has been through eighteen too many washes,
I know this piece is a ticking alarm
or bomb
that will burst apart my chest.
And there will be yet another void,
another hole,
gap,
puzzle piece that makes the larger picture haunted with ghosts because it can't be complete.
And so I cling onto this piece,
wood from a sinking ship,
because the only thing I know
is the permanence of impermanence.
And how empty forever feels.

Blood Pleas and Library Books

After fourteen minutes,
they come back,
to me crumpled on the floor
and say I need to look
at an aspiration
at an x ray.

To look eye to eye at the thing that will take you from me.

They give me a deadline,
four to eight weeks.

And I offer every sacrifice the Bible warned me against
for anything longer.

And my blood plea is answered.

For the next six months,
we live at this impasse
of living
and dead
simultaneously.

Like tomorrow doesn't matter
because it's already here.
We've had our return date stamped at the end of our novel,
and now it's just a matter of returning you back to the library.

We eat meals in silence.
I cook more than I used to.
I wear gloves and wash my hands after your meals,
after you puke the medication up
and I shove it back down your throat
because I don't know how tomorrow
works without you.

And then
tomorrow is today

You can't get out of bed.

You collapse getting into the car,
and I plead with bone marrow
every skin fiber of my being
that today is not today.

But it is.

So I play god and force you to wait.

I force you to stay with me,
one more weekend
where we can't make it up and down the stairs anymore
where you refuse to eat
to get out of bed.

And then,
Monday comes.

In The Morning

I don't want to get out of bed.
Don't want to shower.
Don't want to stop for breakfast, coffee, and order two sandwiches.
Don't want to drive to work.
Don't want to sit at my desk.
Don't want to watch the knife of time gut the next seven hours.
Don't want to help you into the car.
Don't want to drive to where we go next.
Don't want to turn right at the stop sign.
Don't want to hear our song on the radio.
Don't want to park the car, crawl into the backseat holding you, liquid pouring down my face.
Don't want to open the door.
Don't want to walk in.
Don't want to hear them tell me I'm making the right choice.
Don't want to feed you treats out of my hand.
Don't want to watch the needle slide in.
Don't want to hear you yelp the second time they miss the vein.
Don't want to feel your body go slack, then stiff.
Don't want to rub your ears until all the warmth drains from them.
Don't want to walk out holding an empty leash, empty harness.
I don't. I don't. I don't.

The Last Moment

I expected to feel it—
the moment where you slipped from this world
to that.
When your breath stopped in your chest,
heart straining for one last beat.
I expected to know when the last
moment was.
Almost like I could hold the ghosts in my hand
and shape them like Play-Doh
so that they would be more gentle welcoming you
and peeling away the best parts of me.
I expected that you would somehow tell me
when the time came
and not leave me alone on the floor.
But like all other important moments
of my life,
this one was stolen
when someone else said that you were gone.

When It's Time

They said
I would know when the time comes.
When I asked what that meant,
they answered, "You'll know."

And as your breathing becomes labored,
as you yelp getting into the car,
as your legs fail you,
I know.

We sit on the steps eating pizza rolls,
I hold you for as long as I can.
You gently wag your tail to say you're okay
that it's time and you'll be fine.

The thing they forget to warn you about,
is that you can know when it's time,
you can know it's the right thing to do,
but just because it is,
doesn't mean you'll ever be ready to let go.

Baxter

The first thing I tell people
when I meet them
is that my dog is dead.

The dog lover's jaws drop.
They tuck me in their arms,
and smother me in similar stories.
They say, *Oh I'm so sorry.*
I lost mine at x y and z years old.

Then there are others,
who look at me like he was just a dog.
Just eleven years of an otherwise incomplete
and unremarkable life.
That his absence in my bed shouldn't matter
because *here's a man to share the mattress with.*

And yet.
They weren't there when my mother came and said, *pack your bags*
we have twenty four hours.
Or when after these hours came,
we left my sister's clothes, and picture frames,
and went to a house
where a man drank until he passed out at the table
during my soap opera.

They weren't there during the summer I considered suicide
because I couldn't make sense of this life
or what comes next.

And then I met a puppy in a parking lot,
and suddenly soccer made sense.

Suddenly, the broken puzzle pieces fit more tightly together,
as though a layer of glue had been added to my otherwise chaotic parts,
and I was no longer colorblind.
I knew what sunlight felt like,
why the world is on an axis and how it spins.

And yet, my dog is dead.
The one who curled around me when I sobbed on a couch

because he felt a heartbeat in me
that wasn't my own.
And I didn't want it there.
But the churches I was raised in,
seeking shelter from abuse and alcohol
told me that removing it was a sin.

And my child is dead.

And my dog is dead.

Because I wasn't sure I could make it down the stairs.
The one who caught me when my foot slipped on a peg
and tumbled me downward.
I should have been hurt.
Twisted an ankle at the very least.
But my dog, that you tell me was just a dog,
caught me,
comforted me,
put my legs beneath me when I was ready to jump.
When I was ready to crash.
When my friends told me the only difference between my driving
and my driving under the influence
was how fast I go.
And so I asked for him to have another ride home.

And so now,
my dog is dead.
Because cancer riddled his organs
and though I became clockwork with medications, gloves, appointments,
pulling funds from inside my body to outside,
he fell from my car,
on the way to work.
And I screamed loud enough the construction workers heard me and came running.
I told them I had a magical pill,
because I was told to believe this.
But I was also told that I was only buying time.

And so my dog is dead.
Because on his last day,

he laid in bed when I asked if it was time to go to work.
And he ate treats from my hand as he fell asleep.
And the Starbucks barista held me as I cried.
So.
My dog is dead.
And I don't understand how the earth keeps spinning.

Dear Tinder

Profile picture depicts happy girl—
shows gleaming with teeth earned with four dollar a bottle toothpaste
occasional white strips
and brushing at least twice a day.

Profile pictures depicts well-adjusted girl—
one with her arms thrown wide as though she's inviting the world for a hug,
another where she twists her face in a funny way because she didn't like a joke.
The world is a joke.
Isn't it so funny?

Profile picture depicts girl with dogs.
    Dogs piled on the bed,
    dogs on the couch,
    dogs on top of a mountain, camping…
She smiles with sunglasses on with one beside her in a car.

Profile explains, "I have three dogs.
They all sleep on the bed."

Profile forgets to mention,
    that all these pictures were taken before August 14
    there are only two dogs now.

Profile picture says swipe right
because smiling face with white teeth promises a good time.
    Profile picture promises she's stable
        promises she doesn't sit on my couch at night and cry because
        the day before I put my dog down,
            my sister called to say
            my best friend died, too.

Profile picture and profile text
promises two-dimensional girl.
One that can't harbor grief in her chest
like a ship anchor on a wooden dock that's rotting from the salt.

                Profile begs
                SWIPE RIGHT
        So that I can feel anything other than this.

The Next Appointment

In the morning, I should wake up early enough to complain. I should mix greens in with canned food because I read somewhere that greens help fight cancer. I should run them both out before we leave. I should get in the car still wiping sleep from my eyes, complaining about tired, looking forward to an iced peppermint latte. We should drive an hour, meet with the oncologist, and they should do the ultrasound we pushed off last appointment. They should tell me with soft voices I'm still losing the battle, I'm still only buying time, but *he still looks good*. I should breathe a little. I should be late to work today, should have had to use PTO. Instead, I twist the key to my PO Box, and so many cards read *I am so sorry for your loss.*

Control

If you let it out
this will always pour—
His absence, the night the earth shattered
but only you felt the quake.
And this is why
at all times
you must stay in control,
calm and collected with your hands in your lap
because when they see you

they'll comment how happy you look

how many stitches are holding you together

how long your hair is as though this growth

signifies healing.

They don't see how short you cut your bangs,
don't see the bags under the eyes
don't drink the liquor based bloodstream.

They don't see the car accident
peeling off the roadside.

They say you look happy,
and so you stay sealed in a coffin like control.

Enyo

I wish my puppy could talk to my depression
the way she talks to a trash can.
She jumps up,
knocks it over, not fearing consequence, and finds
whatever smells good.
Even if it's attached to aluminum foil,
she devours the evidence.
I clean up the mess when I get home.

I wish my puppy could talk to my depression
the way she talks to her toys,
gutting them in under thirty seconds,
contents spilling on the floor.
Snowflakes in the middle of July.
She will tear through until she finds the squeaker and silences it
kind of like I wish she could do for the voices in my head.
I clean up the mess when I get to it.

I wish my puppy could talk to my depression
the way she talks to mountains,
climbing boulders and high elevations so quickly
though the leash keeps us together,
I have to scramble after her.
We crawl into bed when we get home to rest.

I wish my puppy could talk to my depression
so that on the days it's hard to get out of bed
hard to go for a walk
hard to brush my teeth
hard to do anything other than lay in bed with a pillow over my head,
she could know I'm sorry

I just can't today.

The World without Them

This is the moment you can't get out of bed
not because it's impossible
but because there is no point.
It is the moment the dark wraps its
dove wings around you.
And stills the throbbing within.
Each
  Beat
   That
    Says
     Why
      Bother?
And so you lay in the black
like your loved one will come back.
And when they don't
and when the sun shines like betrayal
today
tomorrow
and times after that,
it'll feel like an assault to your eyes
because they haven't adjusted
to the world where your person doesn't exist.
And this day somehow manages to be bright
and convince you that it should be happy.
So you take a small step.
You brush your teeth.
You continue going
like your heart is in recovery.
To everyone else, on the surface
you look fine,
but in the black hole surrounding you,
you'll know you're lying.

My Therapist Wants to Hospitalize Me

                                          I think you should go to the hospital.
So I can have my clothes searched.
So I can't lock the bathroom doors again,
so I'll be stuck in that place again.
I tell her no, I won't go again.
I'm doing okay.
Not great.
But okay.
                                                        You're struggling
And I am.

The thoughts that were just thoughts, take form
and my hand grasps the sharper objects near me,
edges pressing into the skin on my fingers
so that there is a dent.
Or how I've been clutching the steering wheel a bit harder.
Sometimes it jerks to the left
when there is a semi nearby.
Sometimes, I can't control it.

But I am okay.
I don't tell her this.
I say,
The hospital won't change anything.
                        It'll be a safe place so you can process your feelings.
My dog is dead.
My best friend is dead.
Within 24 hours of each other.
My chest has been scooped out like an empty carton of ice cream.

I tell her,
These are not feelings to be processed.
When the deaths of friends and family become craters in your soul
that cannot be buried
cannot be ignored
because every aspect of your life has been uprooted by their absence.
*This is not something
a temporary stay will fix or heal.*

                      She sits back in her chair, defeated.
                    So, she asks, *what will you do?*

What I Already Knew

I thought my being existed the way they draw diagrams
in text books;
Two arms, two legs, two feet.
Mark an x for anywhere you feel pain.

But I was unaware that when you
fall in love another appendage forms.
It ties you up like a knitted scarf,
makes you complete like you weren't before.
Sewing your ends nice and tight
so that when you're screaming in the middle of the night,
no one can see where the scissors came
and ripped you away from me.

In those moments where you bow defeat
and wait for the scarring to be complete
those to claim to be your friends
will you push you away
while you're trying to mend.

They can't see the missing parts
the way the beats used to fill your heart.
They just see the car crash,
the broken glass,
and they'll tell you
you don't repair fast.

Fire Hydrants

The picture is so cliché—
a dog walks by and lifts its leg.
You allow it because this is the
natural order of the world.
You think it'll happen again
and again and again and again

Until the day you walk by with an empty leash,
and learn to take different streets
to avoid the god damn fire hydrant.

On Being Happy

I want to tell him about the phone call.
How the world stopped when I put toothpaste on my brush
as I got ready for school.
I want to tell him when I heard the ring,
my blood was colder than a mid-winter lake
because there was an accident the night before
and we were waiting for news.
And sometimes
I am psychic.

I want to tell him about my legs buckling from the weight of answers
the ground opening and swallowing me so ferociously I did not feel the
impact of the floor.
My mother waking to my screams,
"No, no, no!"
I didn't know I was making sound.

I want him to stand beside me at the cemetery
as her mother collapses on her casket,
as a brother collapses on another friends' casket,
as a son collapses on his mother's casket,
as the same people kneel before an urn,
and when I walk into the sterile environment to ask for the remains of my
best friend.

I want him to reach into my chest,
and feel the bumps and bruises on my heart
the craters, gaps, and potholes that will never fill
like an unpaved road
after a wash out.

Each day without them is a stubbed toe,
a bent backward nail,
bent so far the quick bleeds for a few minutes a day.

And he tells me to be happy,
as though happiness is a light switch,
when the phone call said the light bulbs burst.

Because I collect my friends' obituaries the way
school children collect baseball cards.

The Last Touch

My hands have touched this door no less than 1,460 times.
At least once a day.

Add times for moving in—
door held open so my elbows did not slam against the frame
drop the box on my foot, knee, leg, again.

Add times for letting the dogs out and sitting in the yard,
watching the leaves fall from the dying tree
that would later lose its branch in a wind storm and break my windshield.

Add times for forgetting items,
going back inside
left my coffee outside
in and out and in and out,
a revolving merry go round.

From day one there were no plans to stay forever
no plans to settle long enough for bookshelves
or a comfortable king size bed.
We were not meant to stay.

I have touched this door no less than 1,460 times.
I can tell you the gold color against the green backdrop is nauseating.
I can tell you that during a winter storm
the handle will become so cold,
the warmth from your hand will freeze to it, so be sure to wear gloves.
The snow will build around the edge, so at times, you'll have to kick it
to get it to open.
In a rain storm, it will not twist fast enough. Potentially kick again.
In case of emergency, like the time you've forgotten your keys inside,
you learn to card the space between frame and lock.

My hands have touched this door no less than 1460 times.
Add times for emergency veterinarian visits.
Add times for the last day my dog lived.
Add times for—
and today,
Is the last time I will touch it.

On Why I'm Not Better Yet

In two weeks,
it'll have been a year.
But I still say it happened in August
as though August is twelve hours ago.

Because I still swallow moments like my foot is caught on a rock in the river.
Because I can still feel the fibers in my hand as they turned cold.
Because I can still feel the ache in my chest
that for two weeks I took as heart complications.

You were a corkboard and I was a thumbtack, grounded
for seven years.
You were gravity that kept me from floating off into space.
You were the other half of my being.
When I fell, you caught me.
When I cried, you held me.

You knew everything and all you asked was that I don't leave you again.

        So I didn't.

I stayed the night you got sick,
until the evening you didn't wake up,
even though my marrow was cat nails against my skin
begging me to be anywhere but here with you.

I stayed until I oxygen was lake water in my lungs
because your body was stiff.

I stayed until your bones were snow
and my ice hands were fire.

I stayed until you were so still I held my breath just to hope I could give you
one more.

And when you didn't,
I would have sawed off my legs,
sacrificed my hands, my pens, my tongue,
if it meant you'd stay a little longer.

You were something to come home to,

a friend who listened,
the person consistently in my corner
when friends and family vanish like fog days after the rain.
You were the reason to keep going.

And so, when people ask me why I'm not better yet,
I want to tell them my smile has become a graveyard,
my chest a haunted forest,
and my eyes, vacant hotel rooms,
with ghosts pouring out of the walls.
Because you were supposed to live forever,
and forever ended in August.

On Letting Myself Feel

I picked a beer up today/rolled the cold bottle back and forth in my hands/tore at the label just enough the corners dented./It's heavier when it's full/it looks less like poison when it's full/and then I put it back in the fridge./I closed the door/walked back to my couch, and sat down./My dogs didn't have to watch their step/so that they didn't knock over an open bottle./They were able to climb up, rest their bodies against me and fall asleep/without me yelling about a spill/without me having to get up for another drink in ten minutes./I looked through old pictures/the ones where I'm smiling because the world hasn't shattered yet./My eyes were so bright then/so full of that stupid hope that something better would happen tomorrow./And then tomorrow came, and here we are./I watched my best friend's husband leave the church after her funeral./I witnessed his jagged breath when he saw the sunlight,/how he clutched his stylish hat in his hand before taking an unsure step forward./The ground I sat on was concrete./The ground he walked on was something more like wet cement threatening to swallow him/and entomb him alive./Her son played in the dirt that would cover her urn./She is buried atop my sister's best friend./She is also buried beside that friend's mother./I don't understand how the world works./How she died the day before my dog had to be put down./How someone's heart can stop beating after a day at the beach./How grief is the only comfortable home I have ever known/bookshelves full of memories that time and dust continue to erase/and picture frames from moments I thought we'd have more of./The couch is comfortable in the grief, because I've spent hours with mascara running down my face./The cushions know my body, pillow clutched to my chest when oxygen was in short supply./Most of the time, I go to the fridge/open a bottle and pretend like liquid can numb this all away./And today/I put the bottle back./Maybe tomorrow I will too.

When My Sister Calls

My sister calls to ask me
"Why would my dog be bleeding from
 his mouth?"

She asks me because I am a dog person.
She asks me because I have a degree in medical biology
and a life ago planned to become a veterinarian.
She asks me
because I am a black hole of grief,
and I so on cue, I tell her
she has to find where the blood
is coming from.

She doesn't call me for two days.
Doesn't follow up to tell me what she's found
and in the absence of my phone ringing I know
in the way you know.

She puts him down four days later.

Her husband says it was a tumor.
Her son calls me sobbing
gasping for breath saying,
This must have been how it felt when you lost yours.

Kyla

My mother watches my girl
unfurl from the couch and move haphazardly
to the bedroom.

She's slowing down, my mother comments, eyes thick
with store bought sadness.

It's true—
her once lively step is halted,
the fur that frames her face is grey and white.
her eyes have become milky pools.

She is slowing down, I say.
But I have had to let go of a dog
whose life gave out before
his body.

And this—watching her age—watching
her slow, taking more measured steps,
having to help her on the couch, into bed, in the car as
she can no longer twist her hips
to jostle her forward.

This I tell my mother, *This isn't sad, this is a gift, a privilege.*
Getting to watch her go from mountain hiking, tennis ball chasing youth,
to aged walks more pee breaks to the eventual still and
final rest.

Dear Stranger,

You don't know me, but I have loved your dog for the last eight years. She still hates fire alarms after all this time, but can tolerate the ones on TV finally. I never found out what caused the fire, you never told people through the grape vine, and so I never fully understood what all she lived through. I just know that she made it out and her puppies didn't. She hasn't fully healed, and I think that's her right. But she has come so far in the time we've been together.

I can't help but to wonder—how could you let her go so easily?

She has licked the salt marshes from my face. It's hard to keep crying when a sixty-five-pound pit bull won't stop licking your face from chin to forehead. She feels it is her duty—to stop me from crying. I've had to tell her, that it's an okay thing to do from time to time.

And you, handed the leash over.

I want you to know it took nearly a year for us to fall in love. It happened when she found me laying on the bathroom floor, shaking and whimpering from a migraine. She licked my face and laid with me for twelve straight hours. She didn't even ask to go outside and go potty.

You see, she got heartworm when she was with you. You never treated her, and so by the time I could afford to take her to the vet, it was fairly advanced. We chose the arsenic treatment—the most aggressive. So she laid, and whimpered, and shook for weeks while she went through it. So, she found me on the floor, and I think maybe she assumed I was going through the treatment, too. She's an old lady dog now—not only slowing down, but grey face and eyes that pool more milk by the day. She has two types of cancer, and Cushing's disease. Her body is tired, and I know she'll leave me soon. I thought, maybe, you'd want to know.

I guess all of this is to say—
    Dear Stranger,
    I adopted your dog.
    And I have loved her as long as I could.

An Ode to the First Dead Pet

On the day you tell me your cat died,
you go on to say that this is the first loss
you've experienced as an adult.

Too many times we are told
I am so sorry for your loss.

This sentiment should be reserved for the pets
who we do not get to hold at the end,
to offer one final pat, thank you, goodbye to.

There is magic in
holding a friend for years,
sharing the bed with them,
then, helping to ease the passing
from here to there.

Instead of *I'm sorry,* I tell you
Congratulations—
because this is a moment to be grieved
and also celebrated,
not apologized for.

There is some ownership in being *adult enough*
to hold a life for years,
be each other's companion,
and make the final call
for the first time.

To You, Before Your Loss

I do not envy what you'll go through—
the stages of grief that come before the actual loss.
The diagnosis, and if not that, the understanding that life is no longer permanent
nor promised.

But along this journey I wish you this—
cloudy eyes from mountain tops where the sky touches the sea,
blankets of ocean tackled by sand,
and everything in between.

I wish you—
Slower walks that remind you to catch your breath,
days that lead to longer naps by your side.

Above all these things,
I wish you old age—
A grey face and arthritic bones,
and the grace to brace for the inevitable,
no matter how this moment comes to you.

And at the end
peace.

With Thanks:

If you're holding this collection, it is likely that you have lost a fur friend of your own, and for that, my deepest condolences. It is one of the most difficult things I have experienced, and I do not wish this grief on anyone. Perhaps our loves are playing together at the rainbow bridge? Thank you for holding this work, and for supporting it. I hope it has helped you to know you are not alone in your grief.

This collection wouldn't have come into being without the loss of the greatest love and soulmate I've ever known, Baxter. Adopted in 2006, he spent the next four years in the care of my aunt and uncle in Massachusetts until I stole him back after Thanksgiving in 2010. We spent the next seven years together, moving from the Outer Banks, NC to the winter wonderland of Maine. In 2017, he was diagnosed with hemangiosarcoma—a terminal diagnosis, two weeks after my girl, Kyla, was diagnosed with a sarcoma. The veterinarians expected him to only make it four more weeks….he stayed with me for close to six months, and I will forever be thankful for that.

That said, thank you to Heather Beatty, who when I was debating whether or not to take him back from my aunt, quelled my worry by saying, "You won't know what you'll be capable of until you take him. Stop worrying. Get him, and figure it out."

Thank you to MB for teaching me to take all the photos, all the videos, and to call the oncologist when my original vet told me to give up. I owe Baxter's last five months to you, and there aren't enough words I can offer to thank you appropriately.

Thank you to everyone I called sobbing the night of the diagnosis. Special thanks to Roy Hargreaves for being with me that night and so many others, Colton Cyr, Emily Robinson for being there on the last night, and Mama P and Papa P for all the times I called crying, and for helping support me during that awful time period. Thank you to my mom who handed me beers without question every time she saw me crying. Thank you to LaUra Schmidt and everyone who donated to Baxter and Kyla's GoFundMe after the diagnosis's.

Thank you to all the employers I've ever had who let me bring Baxy to work, even if only occasionally. Thank you to Matt Gilliam who handled Baxy's meds on more than one occasion, Jon Costa for Baxter's last good weekend, and a place to stay before and after. Thank you to Amy, the kind Starbucks barista who held me as I cried when I ordered Baxter's last pup cup. You were an angel that day. Thank you to Marlene and Eric who met me outside the clinic and held me while I sobbed until I was safe to drive home.

Thank you to Portland Veterinary Specialists, especially Dr. Gail Mason, for their care of my boy, as well as the pharmacist at Scirx Pharmacy. Your compassion and support meant the world to me. Thank you to my therapist and primary care physician at the time. I know I worried you. Truth be told, I worried me, too. But I'm still here.

Thank you to the random dudes from Tinder who helped distract me for short periods of time during this loss. Sorry I used most of you for food and weed.

Thank you to the people who helped me write this collection: Maya Williams, Jessie Tweedie, Alex Ruiz, Patrick McDonald. Thank you all for your support, your guidance, all of it.

Thank you to anyone who has ever loved a dog.

Finally—thank you to anyone who loved Baxter.

Additional Acknowledgments

Thank you to *Crepe and Penn*, Halcyone Publishing, *Royal Rose*, Frost Meadow Review, *Poets of New England*, She Will Speak Series—*I'M NOT CRAZY*, and *Empty Mirror* which published Dear Tinder, Aftermath, Road Map, Baxter, Enyo, How Forever Feels, My Therapist Wants to Hospitalize Me, and When My Sister Calls in varying forms.

Baxter received the Editor's Choice Award from Frost Meadow Review, and Baxter and Road Maps were nominated for 2019 Best of the Net. Blood Pleas and Library Books was a 2019 PNWA Literary Contest Finalist.

Thank you to Andrea Gibson and Megan Falley for helping generate the prose poem, Dear Stranger, as well as the Ode to The First Dead Pet, and An Ode to the Cancer that will Take My Dog, during the Write Your Heart In workshop.

Thanks to the Murphy Writing Poetry and Prose Getaway 2019 which generated the poems, When You Try and Pray this Away, and The Reoccurring Nightmare Where You Won't Be Able to Save Them.

SAFTA Writing Residency for giving me the space to help generate the poems, On How Dogs Choose Their People, Kyla, When He Screams Long Enough A Local Domestic Abuse Survivor Gets Text Reading, "Are You Safe?"

www.ingramcontent.com/pod-product-compliance
Lightning Source LLC
LaVergne TN
LVHW041550070426
835507LV00011B/1027